SAM'S BUMPER JUMPER

World

In Pontypandy High Street there is a small café owned by a very nice Italian lady called Bella.

Bella is good and kind, and loves doing things for other people. Today she is knitting a jumper for Fireman Sam.

"It's-a-going to be a big-a-surprise for Sam," she said to Rosa, her little furry kitten.

DING! went the doorbell as someone came into the café. Bella put down her knitting and went out to serve the customer.

It was 'Elvis' Cridlington. "Tea and toast please, Bella," he said.

Bella made the tea and toast, put them on Elvis's table, and went back into the parlour to carry on knitting.

"Now let-a-me-see," she said. "Where was I up-a-to . . ." She had forgotten how many rows she had done. Was it-a-fifty two or-a-twenty five? she wondered.

"I'd-a-better be on the safe-a-side," she said to Rosa, "and call it-a-twenty five."

She started knitting ferociously, her needles a positive blur! But then . . . *DING!* another customer had come into the café. Bella sighed and put down the knitting.

"I'll-a-never get it finished at-a-this rate," she sighed.

This time it was Trevor Evans. He sat down at the table with Elvis and asked Bella for toasted teacakes and hot chocolate.

When Bella had made Trevor's snack, she went back into the parlour to knit some more of Sam's jumper.

Disaster had struck the woolly jumper!

"Mama mia!" shouted Bella. "You-a-naughty pussycat!"

Rosa was rolled up in a huge tangled pile of wool. She was looking very guilty indeed.

Bella picked up the remains of the jumper and tried to untangle it.

What am I-a-going to do with-a-this? she thought. It didn't take long to untangle the wool and roll it back into balls, but then . . .

"Mama mia," she sighed. "Where was I up-a-to? Was it-a-eighty two or-a-twenty eight?"

"I'd-a-better be on the safe side," she said to Rosa, "and-a-call it-a-twenty eight."

Her needles flew into action and Sam's woolly jumper started to grow.

Bella had just put the very last stitch in the jumper when the café bell rang. Bella bustled out to see who had come into the café this time.

It was Fireman Sam with Sarah and James.

"Ah, cara mia!" said Bella with a great big smile. "It's-a-my two favourite children." She gave them a big hug and then turned to Sam. "And-a-my favourite fireman. I have something extra special for you, Sam."

Sam backed away nervously, thinking that Bella was going to give him a big hug, too! But it was something entirely different.

Bella rushed into the parlour and came out carrying a huge parcel, which she handed to Sam.

"It's-a-for you," she said with a smile.

"What is it, Uncle?" asked James, as Sam took the parcel from Bella.

"Please open it quickly, Uncle Sam," begged Sarah, "and see what is inside."

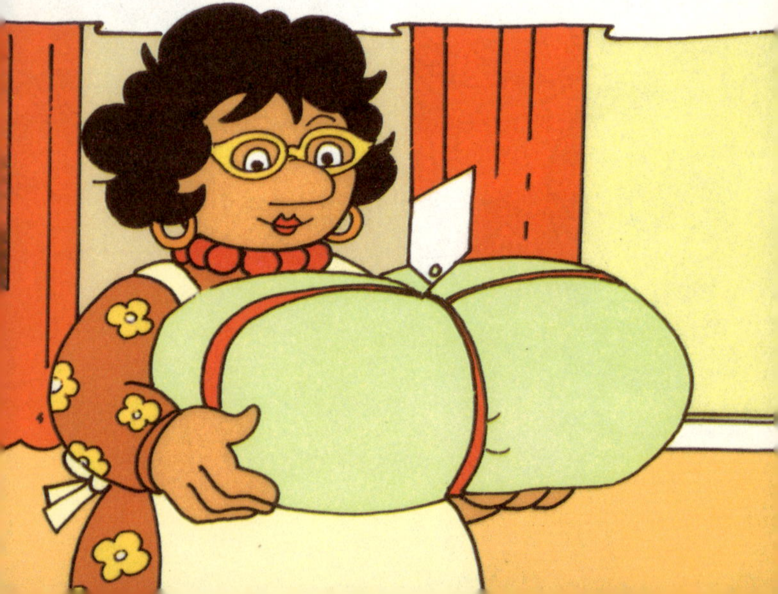

Sam quickly stripped away the paper and pulled out the woolly jumper.

"Oh, it's beautiful!" gasped Sarah. "Try it on right away, Uncle Sam." Sam pulled the jumper over his head . . . and everyone stared in amazement.

"I think it might be just a little bit biggish," said James finally.

"Mama mia," wailed Bella. "What have I done?"

"Who did you use as a pattern, Bella?" asked Elvis Cridlington. "King Kong?"

"Don't be cruel, Elvis," snapped Sarah. "It's a very nice jumper."

"It's all-a-my fault," said Bella sadly. "I'm-a-hopeless!" She put her head in her hands and started to sob quietly.

"Don't cry, Bella," said Fireman Sam. "I really like it."

"You do?" asked Bella, brightening up a bit, but before Sam could answer, Station Officer Steele came into the café.

"What are you doing in the elephant rug, Sam?" he asked.

"WAAAHHHH!" wailed Bella, tears pouring from her eyes like rain drops.

"I've said the wrong thing, haven't I?" said Station Officer Steele, as everyone glared at him.

"You certainly have," said Sarah sternly. "That is Uncle Sam's new jumper, knitted specially by Bella."

"Oh!" gulped Steele. "Sorry Bella . . . it's very nice . . . roomy too . . ."

Further conversation was stopped by a flash of lightning, followed immediately by a huge clap of thunder. *BOOOOMMMMM*. Sam almost jumped out of his jumper with fright.

Then the telephone started to ring.

Bella picked up the telephone and listened for a second. "It's-a-for you," she said, handing the receiver to Station Officer Steele.

Steele listened intently, a grim look on his face. "Don't worry," he said. "We're on our way!"

"What's happened, Mr Steele?" asked James.

"Lightning has struck the church spire," replied Steele, "and it's beginning to burn. Let's go, men!"

The firemen rushed outside and jumped into Jupiter, the fire engine. Sam started the engine and they roared off to deal with the emergency.

The vicar was waiting anxiously for them, and as Jupiter screeched to a halt at the church he pointed to the top of the church spire. The lightning had made a big hole just below the weather cock.

"The fire hose will be no use here," said Station Officer Steele. "Someone will have to go up the ladder and put out the blaze with an extinguisher. I need a volunteer!"

"It's a long way up, isn't it?" said Elvis, looking at the top of the spire high above them.

"A very long way up," said Trevor Evans nervously.

"Well, naturally I would go," said Steele, "but as fire chief, I have to be in control here on the ground."

"I could go, I suppose," said Elvis, "but my new shoes would be ruined."

"And I can't go up," said Trevor, "because . . . because . . ." He thought for a moment and then smiled. "Because I want to give Sam the opportunity to go up the ladder!"

"Thanks very much!" said Sam grumpily.

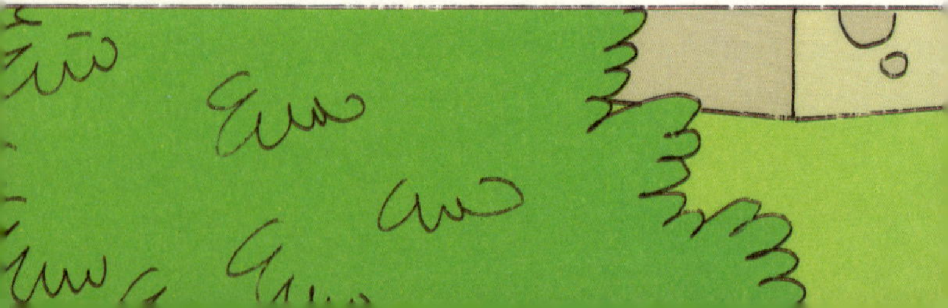

Sam picked up the fire extinguisher and started the long climb up the ladder.

It seemed to take ages to get to the top, but finally he was able to look into the hole and see the fire.

"I am going to put out the fire now," he shouted to the others on the ground.

Lifting up the extinguisher, he pressed the button, and a jet of foam shot out to smother the flames. The fire was quickly put out.

Then things started to go wrong!

Sam was just about to climb down the ladder when a large bird flew down and perched on his nose.

"OUCH!" yelled Sam, as the bird's long talons gripped his nose firmly, bringing tears to his eyes.

"Ged off by dose immediately!" he shouted. But the bird had decided that Sam's nose made the perfect perch. He was *not* going to be moved off easily.

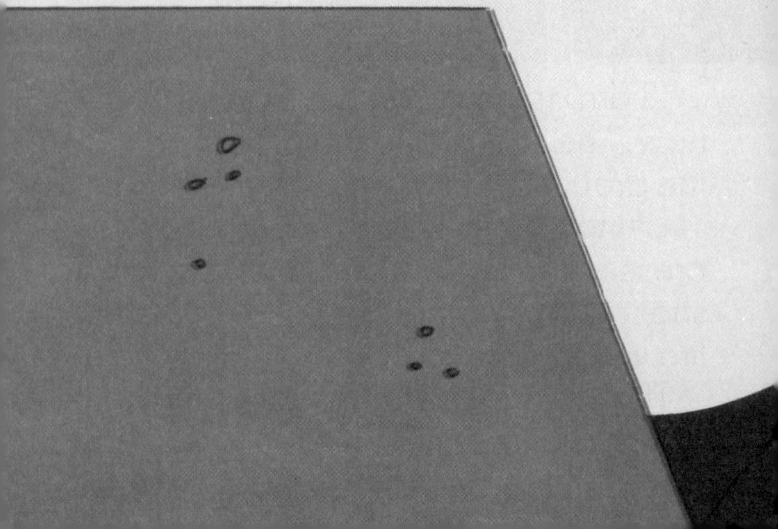

The next thing to go wrong was that Sam accidentally dropped the fire extinguisher.

"I think Sam has dropped the fire extinguisher," said Elvis Cridlington, looking up.

"So he has," agreed Station Officer Steele.

"I think it's going to hit us," observed Trevor Evans.

"HIT US?" they all shouted. "LET'S GET OUT OF HERE!"

They just managed to dive out of the way before the extinguisher hit the ground with a loud THUMP!

"Phew! That was close," said Trevor. The others agreed.

While they were talking, the ladder fell over!

Sam felt the ladder start to slip. Just in time, he managed to leap off and cling tightly to the weather cock.

The bird on his nose decided that all this jumping about was too much trouble and flew away. Sam was very relieved about that. So was his nose!

Then he looked down. "GET ME DOWN FROM HERE!!!!!!!" he yelled.

"The ladder is broken," said Trevor Evans, looking down at the shattered steps.

"That was the longest ladder in Pontypandy," said Station Officer Steele.

"We'll never get Sam down without it!" added Elvis.

They all looked up at Sam.

"Don't worry, Sam," shouted Station Officer Steele. "We'll get you down."

"But how?" asked Trevor Evans.

"How about a helicopter?" suggested Elvis. "A helicopter could pluck him to safety!"

"You've been reading too many comics," said Station Officer Steele. "Besides, the nearest helicopter base is miles away. No . . . we have to think of something simple."

"How about . . ." began Trevor.

"No, that's no good either," snapped Steele impatiently.

"He could dive into a bucket of water," said Elvis. The others looked at him in amazement.

"I read about it once in a comic," admitted Elvis sheepishly.

"Why don't you catch him in a net?" asked a strange voice from behind the hedge. It was the vicar.

"Of course!" said Steele. "Why didn't I think of that?"

"Because you don't read the right kind of comics," muttered Elvis under his breath.

"What was that, Cridlington?" snapped Station Officer Steele.

"Nothing, chief, nothing at all," replied Elvis innocently.

"Hmm," said Steele. "Right, men," he ordered, "get the net!"

"We haven't got one," said Trevor Evans.

"Haven't got one?" echoed Steele. "All firemen have a net!"

"Well we haven't," said Elvis. "We used to have one, but it got used as a fish net when the canal bank burst and we had to rescue the fish."

Then Trevor Evans had a brainwave.

"Wait here!" he shouted, as he leapt into Jupiter and drove swiftly off, leaving Elvis and Steele standing by the church.

Minutes later he was back, with Mrs Price and Norman, Sarah and James, Bella, *and* Sam's giant jumper.

"Everybody stand round the jumper and pull it tight," ordered Station Officer Steele. "Right, Sam!" he shouted to the tiny figure clinging desperately to the weather cock. "JUMP!"

Sam looked down at the scene below. It looked like a handful of ants holding a postage stamp!

"Jump?" he shouted back. "You must be joking!" But at that moment, the large bird that had previously roosted on Sam's nose decided to give it another try.

Sam saw the bird swooping down with talons extended and remembered the awful pain.

"GERONIMOOOOO!" he shouted, as he leapt for his life.

Sam landed safely on the jumper and bounced to the ground.

Looking at the stretched sweater, he said, "It may not have been a very good jumper, Bella, but it is the best trampoline I have ever been on!"